Acting Edition

The Thin Place

by Lucas Hnath

Copyright © 2021 by Lucas Hnath
All Rights Reserved

THE THIN PLACE is fully protected under the copyright laws of the United States of America, the British Commonwealth, including Canada, and all member countries of the Berne Convention for the Protection of Literary and Artistic Works, the Universal Copyright Convention, and/or the World Trade Organization conforming to the Agreement on Trade Related Aspects of Intellectual Property Rights. All rights, including professional and amateur stage productions, recitation, lecturing, public reading, motion picture, radio broadcasting, television, online/digital production, and the rights of translation into foreign languages are strictly reserved.

ISBN 978-0-573-70903-6

www.concordtheatricals.com
www.concordtheatricals.co.uk

FOR PRODUCTION INQUIRIES

UNITED STATES AND CANADA
info@concordtheatricals.com
1-866-979-0447

UNITED KINGDOM AND EUROPE
licensing@concordtheatricals.co.uk
020-7054-7298

Each title is subject to availability from Concord Theatricals Corp., depending upon country of performance. Please be aware that *THE THIN PLACE* may not be licensed by Concord Theatricals Corp. in your territory. Professional and amateur producers should contact the nearest Concord Theatricals Corp. office or licensing partner to verify availability.

CAUTION: Professional and amateur producers are hereby warned that *THE THIN PLACE* is subject to a licensing fee. The purchase, renting, lending or use of this book does not constitute a license to perform this title(s), which license must be obtained from Concord Theatricals Corp. prior to any performance. Performance of this title(s) without a license is a violation of federal law and may subject the producer and/or presenter of such performances to civil penalties. Both amateurs and professionals considering a production are strongly advised to apply to the appropriate agent before starting rehearsals, advertising, or booking a theatre. A licensing fee must be paid whether the title(s) is presented for charity or gain and whether or not admission is charged. Professional/Stock licensing fees are quoted upon application to Concord Theatricals Corp.

This work is published by Samuel French, an imprint of Concord Theatricals Corp.

No one shall make any changes in this title(s) for the purpose of production. No part of this book may be reproduced, stored in a retrieval system, scanned, uploaded, or transmitted in any form, by any means, now known or yet to be invented, including mechanical, electronic, digital, photocopying, recording, videotaping, or otherwise, without the prior written permission of the publisher. No one shall share this title(s), or any part of this title(s), through any social media or file hosting websites.

For all inquiries regarding motion picture, television, online/digital and other media rights, please contact Concord Theatricals Corp.

MUSIC AND THIRD-PARTY MATERIALS USE NOTE

Licensees are solely responsible for obtaining formal written permission from copyright owners to use copyrighted music and/or other copyrighted third-party materials (e.g. artworks, logos) in the performance of this play and are strongly cautioned to do so. If no such permission is obtained by the licensee, then the licensee must use only original music and materials that the licensee owns and controls. Licensees are solely responsible and liable for clearances of all third-party copyrighted materials, including without limitation music, and shall indemnify the copyright owners of the play(s) and their licensing agent, Concord Theatricals Corp., against any costs, expenses, losses and liabilities arising from the use of such copyrighted third-party materials by licensees. For music, please contact the appropriate music licensing authority in your territory for the rights to any incidental music.

IMPORTANT BILLING AND CREDIT REQUIREMENTS

If you have obtained performance rights to this title, please refer to your licensing agreement for important billing and credit requirements.

THE THIN PLACE was first produced by Playwrights Horizons, Inc., New York City. Commissioned by and premiered in the 2019 Humana Festival of New American Plays at The Actor's Theatre of Louisville and workshopped as part of the Jerry A. Tishman Playwrights Creativity Fund, a program or New Dramatists. It was developed at the Colorado New Play Festival, Steamboat Springs, June 2019 by Peter Jay Sharp Theater, New York on 22 November 2019. The performance was directed by Les Waters, with sets by Mimi Lien, costumes by Oana Botez, lighting design by Mark Barton, sound design by Christian Frederickson. The Production Stage Manager was Paul Mills Holmes and Assistant Stage Manager Kasson Marroquin. The cast was as follows:

LINDA . . . . Randy Danson
HILDA . . . . .Emily Cass McDonnell
JERRY . . . . .Triney Sandoval
SYLVIA. . . . . Kelly McAndrew

CHARACTERS
LINDA
HILDA
JERRY
SYLVIA

PERFORMANCE NOTES

Time and space in this play are fluid, taking the lead of Hilda's narration.

Hilda is the only character who ever narrates.

Ellipses suggest a pause, perhaps a moment where the character is thinking.

Within lines, dashes that join together sentence fragments indicate that the fragments should be run together, without break.

Dashes at the end of a line suggest that a character is being cut off by the next character's line.

Lines that end without punctuation suggest that there should be no air between the finished line and the next one.

Slashes indicate the point at which the next line should overlap.

Question marks – or the lack thereof – are very important. If the line asks a question but does not end in a question mark, be mindful not to inflect it as though it is a question. (This is especially important when Linda conducts her "reading".)

Also, the audience member that Hilda talks to is not a "plant". What they experience with Hilda, they really experience.

PRODUCTION NOTES

The Thin Place includes two stage illusions: a piece of mentalism and a vanish effect. The illusions occur on pages 69 and 74. Licensees are given access to the designs and explanations from the original Illusion Designer, Steve Cuiffo, for a mandatory performance fee. Please reach out to your licensing representative for further information.

THANKS

Robin Bartlett, Reza Behjat, Andrew Boyce, Steve Cuiffo, Randy Danson, Carol Fishman, Adam Greenfield, Kathleen Hefferon, Sue Jean Kim, Andrea Hiebler, Mia Katigbak, Arthur Kopit, Sarah Lunnie, Kelly McAndrew, Emily Cass McDonnell, Bruce McKenzie, Emily Moler, Drew Morrison, Emily Morse, Andres Osorio, Linda Powell, Keith Reddin, Jessica Reese, Kristen Robinson, Noah Rubenstein, Triney Sandoval, Tim Sanford, Jim & Lori Steinberg, Emily Tarquin, Amy Wegener, Taylor Williams, Susan Yassky, and Mona Pirnot.

*Dedicated to
Les Waters and to the memory of Ricky Jay*

HILDA & LINDA

*(There's really not much on stage. Two chairs and a side table between then, that's all. When the play begins, **HILDA** enters. She's in her late thirties. She's carrying a mug of tea. She sits in one of the chairs. The house lights don't dim. They won't dim. Not for some time. She considers the audience. Sips her tea.)*

HILDA. There's that thing where you've been
thinking about someone and then
you start seeing them everywhere –
or you think you're seeing them...

I'm having that right now, with my
grandmother – it's just the funniest thing...

(To various audience members.)

...like I look at you
and I think you look like her...
and I sort of see it with you –
and actually...actually
you look a lot like my grandmother – oh I wish I had a
picture I'd show you –

but no I was just thinking about her the other day
and about this thing she'd do with me when I was little,

where she'd sit with me on the floor
and she'd take her little notepad
and she'd write down a word on it – she
wouldn't show me the word – she'd just

hold the notepad close to her chest,

and she would tell me that she was going to try to send that word into my mind.

She'd say: *all you have to do is listen,*
and when you listen,
you're going to listen
not with your ears,
but with this part here,
just behind and just a little above
your eyes.

She'd say: *Do you understand?*

I'd nod my head.

And then she'd look at me,
and she'd say *I'm sending the word to you.*

And I'd say a word,

and she'd say *no.*

She'd say: *you're not listening.*

And I'd try to listen.

I'd say another word,
and she'd say, no, don't guess.
Just listen.
Just…

…and she'd pick these just completely random words,
words you could never guess.
Like – I don't know – kumquat
or spiral
or…trapezoid.

Because, she didn't want it to be by accident,
she wanted to know that I really could
hear her thoughts.

My mother walked in on us doing this once.
Oh she got so upset – she yelled at her,
she yelled: *what are you doing bringing that
demonic activity into our house,
bringing demonic spirits into our home,
teaching my daughter these*
– I don't know – *demonic things*, you know.

I mean she never even liked grandma all that much –
and eventually – eventually she would
tell my grandmother
no more, no more,
you're not allowed to come into this house,
you're not allowed to see my daughter,
you're not allowed – this and that.

But before all of that, before she was "banished,"
we did – we got very good at it.
Our little game.

Could sometimes even get almost a whole sentence.
And I have no idea if it was real – was I
really hearing her thoughts in the space
just behind and a little above my eye?
Or was it something else.
Did I just get good at guessing,
guessing the kinds of words and thoughts and…
Now my grandmother – she said
that what she was doing was – and my mother
really would <u>not</u> have liked <u>this</u> –
was that what she was doing was getting me ready
for the day she died.

And that if we got really really good at
hearing each other's thoughts like this,
then when my grandmother died, someday,
she would still be able to talk to me.
She'd be able to send words to me from beyond the grave.
Just like you know how you pick up a phone and say
hi how are you –

hope you're well –

trapezoid –

    (Laughs.)

...

But you know, the thing about these little games I
played with my grandmother – those little...
they sort of opened up a door
for me – a door
to this
"other place," this – I don't know what to call it –
this...
thin place(?)

This place where the line between this world
and some other world is
very
thin(?)

Like it's sort of like if you were to imagine an octopus

in an aquarium

pressed up against glass

...except that there's no glass

and no octopus

...

Not long after my mother told her to go away,
not long after "the rift,"
as we called it,
grandma did die.
It was a stroke,
I think.

My mother was never quite the same after that,
and things got really – I don't know – difficult, and
I'd find myself wishing I could talk to my grandmother, so

I'd go up into my bedroom,
after my mother was asleep –
I'd take a candle,
I'd turn off the lights,
and I'd close my eyes,
and I'd open up the
eye that's inside my head – the eye just behind here –
and I'd open it, and I'd ask for grandma.
I'd ask, "grandma?
hello?
are you there?"
And I'd hear things, sure.
And I'd sometimes even feel things,
soft things,
on the back of my neck.
And I'd smell smoke because the candle had gone out.
And I'd just scare myself silly,
because I'd have my eyes closed
and I'd be so scared of what would happen
if I opened them.
Who'd be there?
Would someone be there, staring back at me?
And would it be grandma,
or something else?
And I'd just sit there in the dark until…

until I'd fall asleep,
just too scared to open my eyes until morning.

It's because of my interest in this sort of thing
that I met Linda.
I first met Linda at the start of last year, just
a few months after my mother had
gone missing...
died –? gone missing –?

    (Shrugs.)

Linda was a psychic –
a real professional psychic.

I first met her at something called a "sitting"
which is something that's sort of like
what I did alone in my room as a kid,
but it's done by someone who really
knows what they're doing.

And it takes place at a house, like someone's nice house,
and there's a bunch of people there, gathered together
in the living room, and there's candles
and there's incense burning,
and Linda walks into the room and it begins...

> (**LINDA** *enters. She's in her sixties. She sits next to* **HILDA**. *She has a British accent – more working class than posh. Her affect is flat, blunt, no nonsense. She addresses the audience)*

LINDA. Now let's get one thing straight:
There is no death.
When you die you merely pass on
to something else.

What I do is like a radio antennae.

I tune my dial, then all these voices start comin' at me –
– picture twenty or so people all
tryin' to use the same telephone at once –
and I'm the telephone –
it can get very confusing for me, so
I do need your help:
if I say a name and you think it's someone calling for you,
you have to speak up and let me know, otherwise
I move on
and your grandad or your mum or whoever it is
is sad no one picked up the phone, and
I – ha ha – I look like an idiot.

...

While we're waitin' for the spirits to show up,
tell you a funny story:

This posh lady come to me once
wantin' to know if her deceased husband
had ever cheated on her.

I say *why do you want to know that dear –*
She says, *well since he died, I been
hearin' things from friends –
got me to wonderin'.*

I tell her, *you understand, I can't see what happened,
I'm not a fortune teller, dearie – I just
hear what the spirits tell me,
an' unless the spirit tells it to me, I can't know it –
what makes you think
he'd own up to fucking about.*
But she wouldn't take no for an answer.
So, I set myself to listenin',
had no idea if I'd even be able to reach 'im –
an' honestly was sorta hope'n I wouldn't – because
fact is, you see,

after they pass over the spirits got
nothin' more to fear which means
a lot of them become very, uh, truthful.

After a little bit of waitin' I do – I
get a spirit named Henry. I say
that 'im? She says yes. Ask a few questions
to make sure it's 'im –
It's 'im.
So I go ahead an' ask:
Henry, did you cheat on your wife here.

– well not only did he cheat, but
it wasn't with just one lady –
It was five, seven different ones – the last
bein' the wife's sister.

So, anyway,
that's your warnin', a'right?
Don't ask me a question you don't want an answer to,
because I can't promise it's going to be
the answer you want.
But most spirits, all they want is to
just say hello,
tell you they miss you,
sometimes there's a warnin',
sometimes – oh, here it comes

– come at me like a wave.

Give me a moment...

HILDA. *(To audience.)* ...Linda spoke to
so many spirits that evening.
She would hear a name, say it,
and every time someone would raise their hand
and say that's my brother or
that's my wife or – there was even

a child – who died in a car accident –
she knew the color of the car and where it happened –

LINDA. I'm hearin' a name…

…please speak up spirit…?

…

I think it's Helen – is that it… Helen?
…yes –
who knows Helen.

HILDA. I do

LINDA. *(To* **HILDA.***)* You know Helen.

HILDA. mm-hm

LINDA. someone close to you, passed on, she's –

HILDA. *(To* **LINDA.***)* Yes

LINDA. uh-huh – What's your name dear?

HILDA. Hilda

LINDA. Helen, I've got Hilda here…

…

Helen's your gran, dearie?

HILDA. What –?

LINDA. she your gran – your /grandma

HILDA. yes, she –

LINDA. Passed over recently?

…

no – that's not right –

she's saying it's further back –
when you were a young girl – gettin' like age eight or –

HILDA. mm-hm

LINDA. an' she's rememberin' you in a
bright yellow dress, with straps
like that tied around here – remembers you
wearin' that dress
around the house, in the summer, you remember that

HILDA. yes

LINDA. good – who's Betty?

HILDA. ...

LINDA. Helen's sayin' somethin' about
someone named Betty –
or is it Beth... Sounds like Betty –
Who is that

HILDA. I don't know

LINDA. she doesn't know who that is, Helen – Did
some object go missing recently, something valuable –
something like a bracelet but not a bracelet...

HILDA. no

LINDA. let it pass then – there's someone named Jack.
Who's that –

HILDA. her brother

LINDA. passed on

HILDA. /mm-hm

LINDA. she's telling me that Jack is there with her, and –
and well she's also sayin' that Betty's there too – but no
one here knows who that is, Helen. We've got to move
past Betty, right –? Keeps talking about Betty...

...

I'm getting that there was some sort of...turbulence
surrounding her passing –
What happened in April?

HILDA. April is when she left, I think –

LINDA. passed over –?

HILDA. no –

LINDA. *(Still, to* **HILDA.***)* your gran's not talking about passing over, dearie – she's talking about leaving somewhere, in April – where did she leave –

HILDA. our house

LINDA. Helen's saying she lived with you,
with you and your family

HILDA. yes

LINDA. for awhile

HILDA. yes

LINDA. and then something pushed her away, am I hearing that right

HILDA. there was a fight

LINDA. she's just referring to it as family trouble

HILDA. yeah, that sounds like her

LINDA. and she thinks you felt like you were to blame for it

HILDA. yeah

LINDA. the two of you had a real bond, a real – closeness of spirit

HILDA. mm-hm, that's right, we did

LINDA. ...

...
now she's talking about cause of death.
– Spirits do that, talk about the

circumstances surrounding their death
because they think it provides some comfort to the living.

...

She says it was a stroke...
...I'm gettin' that there were two, strokes.

First one she had, she was with Denise.

>   (*To* **HILDA**.)

Is that family or is that a friend –

HILDA. I think it was a friend of hers

LINDA. says she was with Denise and Albert.
They called the ambulance, and that's
how she ended up in hospital.
And then, there was second stroke
shortly after midnight –
she says, *I felt a tightness of chest,
hard to swallow,
breathing stopped, I knew this was it...
and then it was light, my love, it was all light –
and all disease was gone,
and I was somewhere else...*
'an she wants you to know that family trouble,
that's in the past
and she wants you to know none of it was your fault –

HILDA. okay

LINDA. – says you carry too much,
an' it separates you from the world
and from other people – Look at me dear, look at me –
Sometimes you get a bit lonely don't you

HILDA. mm-hm?

LINDA. she doesn't want you to be lonely,
she wants you to open yourself up to others,
even though it's difficult,

because she wants a full life for you. A'right?

HILDA. thank you

...

can I ask a question

LINDA. yes, my dear, what is it

HILDA. ...

LINDA. go on

HILDA. I was wondering if
my mother...
is she also where my grandmother is –

LINDA. let me ask.

What's her name?

HILDA. Mary.

LINDA. Right – Helen...do I still have you?

...

Helen, is your daughter Mary there.

...Is she there with you.

...

...

Sorry, my dear, no she's not with your gran.
She recently passed...?

HILDA. yes. I think. mm-hm

LINDA. not getting anything.
But that doesn't mean one thing or another –
the world beyond this one has many layers.

Not like the spirits are all

sittin' in a room with each other – ha ha –
you see. Maybe some other time we reach her, right?

That's a dear.

HILDA. Linda was amazing.
She just did what she did so easily and I was just so...
People started leaving, but I just sort of stayed around,

and almost as if Linda could tell what I was thinking,
she walked over to me and said

LINDA. the place where I'm staying
is just around the corner.
Would you come up for a nightcap.

HILDA. And I said, yes.
And that's how Linda and I started
spending time with each other.

I'd never met anyone like her.
I wanted to be near her all the time
and so we'd just sit with each other on her couch,
drink tea and eat cookies, and she'd
tell me all about her childhood in England –

LINDA. had no money, there was eight of us kids,
and what made it worse was
none of us liked each other –

HILDA. Linda loved telling stories and she could easily go on for hours –

LINDA. – always felt I was special though on account of my affliction –

HILDA. she was like a character out of a book from another time – she even had
a mysterious illness –

LINDA. problem with my lungs, ever since I was

a kid – where I seize up, can't breathe, inside it feels
like stabbin' pains – No one can explain it, not
asthma said the doctor. Auntie Panana would say
I was puttin' it on for the attention –
but she was a piece of shit.

HILDA. and I loved listening to her stories because they really were so interesting and always helped to take my mind off things –

LINDA. – had this one aunt and uncle – Auntie Doris an' Uncle John – they'd just fight and scream at each other all hours of the day – <u>her</u> always threatenin' <u>him</u> that if he didn't make more money, she'd go off and get her own job. She'd yell: *John, you're as useless as a spare prick at a wedding.* An' he'd shout right back at her, *Shut yer evil yammering gob you foul mouthed cunt* – ha ha ha – they'd go back and forth like that – just the most horrible people.

But then she did get herself a job – course that just infuriated John – An' to make matters worse – job Doris got herself was way out in Sleaford – nearly a seventy-minute drive from where we lived – an' because they had only one car between 'em, she told John she'd be takin' car, an' he'd have to find some other way to get around.

Now Uncle John – he was never the most stable person, and we had gone in and out of worryin' about him – more than one occasion he threatened to top himself – but who hasn't done that when emotions got the best of 'em –

HILDA. mm-hm

LINDA. and we – well – we just figured that Auntie Doris is no walk in the park either, so – but truth be told I don't think anyone expected how much Doris gettin' herself a job would upset him.

No I think John took a lot of pride in
his ability to provide for Doris,
and he was probably 'fraid that she'd leave 'im if
she found she could do better by herself.
– Also you can't underestimate just pure hatred.
John hated Doris,
and he wanted her to feel just as awful about life
as he felt every single day.

So what he did was he fashioned himself a noose,
a good strong noose
made out of cable, put the noose round his neck, and
tied the other end to the underside of their
car – she had no idea, no idea at all that
he was under the car, waitin',
noose around his neck and piss drunk out of his mind.

And when she went off that morning for her
first day of work at her new job –
well – you can imagine what happened –
dragging poor John all the way to Sleaford –
but no, she didn't actually make it to Sleaford –
someone stopped her well before she got to work.
But Uncle John he was pretty well mangled –
not entirely dead, yet,
but definitely mangled when she stopped the car
to see what all the fuss was about.

You'd have thought that what happened
would have scarred us,
but to be honest, this sort of thing
was always happening in my family.
Life was so hard that you never quite felt it.

You know what I mean, Hilda?

(LINDA *takes* HILDA*'s hand and strokes it gently...*)

I have a feeling you do.
That's what I like about you.

HILDA. ...I started to feel so comfortable with Linda that I started to tell her more about myself, just like she'd told me about herself.

I didn't tell her everything, because I wasn't sure that would be a good idea – my mother would always tell me when I was little, *Hilda you tell people too much – some things you keep to yourself, some things you don't say out loud because if you do, people won't want to be around you* – and this was always a lesson I could never seem to learn – but Linda seemed different, and so I did – I did tell her about my grandmother and the little games we'd play, and about the things I'd do in my bedroom, late at night with all the lights turned off. And how, I could never quite seem to reach my grandmother even though we practiced it, and how what I really wanted to do was what Linda did –

but Linda never really liked talking about her work – she sort of went out of her way to avoid it, so every time I'd bring it up she'd say

LINDA. oh I don't want to talk about work, I'm resting now.

HILDA. I just thought it was strange there was this thing she could do that was really something special, but she wouldn't talk about it with me, and it made me wonder if there was something wrong with me –

LINDA. no, it's just not that interesting is all

HILDA. but I did think it was interesting and I had so many questions – and I did – I asked her if she could call my grandmother again, but she told me she couldn't because we were friends and she can't do it with friends, so I asked her if she could teach me how

to do it myself, but she said, no, so I asked her how she
learned to do it, and how she realized she could do it,
and if it took practice; and I asked her what the spirits
sound like – do they sound more like voices or more
like feelings, and can you hear it like it's in your ear or
does it sound like it's inside your head –

I even once suggested that maybe sometime we just try
seeing what happened if we lit a few candles, and sat
together in the dark – to see what would happen if we
just called on the spirits, together, just once, just please,
just once, just once and I'll never ask again, I'll never –

LINDA. Hilda.

Hilda.

...You do realize don't you that what I do
is sort of a trick, right?

no, what I do sits somewhere between the real
and the unreal – how like a metaphor works –
you know what I mean.

HILDA. I didn't

LINDA. I just sit there and say whatever pops into my head
and let the person sittin' across from me turn it into
somethin'.

HILDA. ...

LINDA. – so like how I start with a name –
I think of names, I say 'em an'
people stop me when I say a name they know –

an' after I figure out who it is I'm s'posed to be talkin' to
I start makin' guesses about them –
things they did in life,
little details, images – *your dad's*

talkin' about a sail boat,
why's he goin' on about that, or –
your husband's tellin' me he
had cancer of the bowel –

Some things I guess right,
some things I guess wrong – no one
remembers the bits I get wrong – so I
just keep makin' guesses
until I get a few things right – and once I do, they will –
people'll go and make just the most
wonderful meaning of it all –

– like the other day got this old fella,
I said to *'im, spirit's sayin' somethin' about a cat –*
What's this cat – he says I don't know,
I say, *did you have a cat when you were a little lad –*
he says no, *but you have one now* – no.
So I add another something else thinkin' that'll jog his –
I say, *no, spirits' sayin' there was a cat that was put down –*
sick cat, had to be put down.

And I wait.

An' I see 'im thinkin' turnin' it over – an' finally he says
It's Kat –
not a cat –
my sister Kat, sister <u>Kathy</u> –
he says, *we had to take her off of life support –*
no one knew what to do – it was me who said we should
take her off –
I did it, I had her die. I killed her.
An' I say, *No my dear, no no my dear, all I can hear*
is the sound of this spirit sayin': Thank you.
Thank you for takin' me out of my sufferin',

Thank you – I know it was hard my dear brother – but you did the right thing.

Do ya get it?

HILDA. I guess

LINDA. It's really not all that different from
that so-called psychotherapy,
except what I do actually works
take some little pudgy girl with greasy hair –
and she's lost her father, and her father
never said a kind word to her
and I can see plain as day what's happening –
so when I tell her
that her father is so very proud of her,
and sees the beautiful woman she's become, and
though he knows that he never
found the words to say it when he was alive,
he wants her to know that he
loves her more than anything –
The sight of – the tears streaming down her face –
the transformation that's happening,
right there in front of my eyes…

because if you have the chance to
bring peace to someone in pain,
it would be cruel – just absolutely <u>cruel</u> not to do it.

Right?

HILDA. uh-huh

LINDA. so that's what I do – nothing to it, really –
but isn't that what's so lovely about it –
any magic there is has nothin' to do with me – no it
happens in them – happens inside of their – it's in them.
It's in you. It's in all of us – ha ha –

I'm so tired, lovey – let's tuck ourselves in for the night, a'right?

HILDA. And Linda went off to bed,
but I didn't follow her.

...now I won't say I was disappointed
when Linda told me about her work,
about how she sorta made it sound more like a "trick"
than – I don't know – some kind of –
something bigger than a trick...

And I won't say that I felt cheated, no,
I definitely did not feel that way.
No, I just felt – um –
I felt –

...and then I heard a strange sound coming from her bedroom

        Linda...?

                ...Are you okay?

    (**LINDA** *starts breathing strangely.*)

I went into her bedroom...
and saw Linda on the floor...

and it looked like she was having trouble breathing...

like she was having one of those breathing spells she had told me about

from back from when she was a kid...

...

I wasn't sure if –

was there something I should do to help...?

could she even tell I was there?

and then it was over.

...she just looked so...scared...

and of course, I felt really bad
seeing her like that,
so helpless,
so weak,

but part of me
also wondered if her having that attack
right when she did
had anything to do with...you know –
her saying certain things about certain things
that maybe she shouldn't be saying...
like maybe there are certain things that it's just dangerous
to talk about...

and who's to say Linda even understood what was
really happening when she did the thing
she called a trick,
because how could she *really* know that a spirit
wasn't actually talking through her
when she'd say names and talk about how people died –
How could she know for sure
where the thoughts were coming from –?
She did know a lot of things about my grandmother
that she couldn't possibly have just guessed.

I don't know.
I just try to keep an open mind about these things.
My mother would always yell at me for that.
She'd say, *Hilda –*
don't you know –

*don't you know you can have such an open mind
that your brain falls out.*

Anyway, after that night Linda started introducing me
to her friends, and it was like – it was like I was part of
some – I don't know – inner circle. I'd never been part of
anyone's inner circle.

I'd be invited to all of Linda's Sunday night get togethers
– where we'd meet at these really nice places, nice houses
and apartments, and there was always really good food,
and really nice wine – expensive stuff where you could
drink a lot without your head hurting too much,

and there'd be the most interesting people there –
these people with job descriptions
that you would ask them what they did
and they would tell you but somehow by the end you felt
like you knew even less than before you asked –

but it was fun – and they all told really fun stories,
and I just liked to listen.

The last one I went to – the last one was actually
a party to celebrate Linda getting her visa.
There had been a problem,
and we all thought that maybe she'd
have to leave the country,
but then it all got figured out and –

That night was just me and Linda
and Linda's cousin Jerry
and this woman Sylvia who Linda was
in some way close with,
I don't know exactly how – just that I
know that Sylvia gave Linda money.
Like they had some sort of arrangement where

Sylvia paid for Linda's rent(?).

...Anyway, that was the last night I ever saw Linda.

LINDA'S PARTY

> *(...A good bit of laughter comes from offstage, and* **LINDA** *laughs too, and* **SYLVIA** *and* **JERRY** *walk on stage –* **SYLVIA** *with wine glasses,* **JERRY** *with wine bottle and corkscrew, mid-chat, having a real great time.)*

JERRY. well, so that reminds me of this thing I saw when I was in Japan

LINDA. now when were you in Japan,/ Jerry –?

JERRY. oh you know back during the uh –
the <u>fallow</u> period/ as I call it – back during the –

LINDA. yes yes Jerry's fallow period

JERRY. I was/ living in Takayama –

SYLVIA. Is everyone drinking? / Does everyone need a –?

LINDA. oh right oh right after that thing with/ – yes Sylvia I think we're fine

JERRY. right, and my friend Randy/ invited me to this thing, this –

SYLVIA. oh I know Randy

JERRY. I don't know what to call it exactly –
it was sort of a party and sort of a performance –
where everyone gathered together in a room,
/about the size of the room we're in right now,
and it's filled with candles, like about fifty candles

LINDA. *(Whispered.)* oh now don't you look fetching Sylvia

SYLVIA. what–? no

LINDA. yes

JERRY. forget it no one's listening/ to me

HILDA. I'm listen/ing

LINDA. we're listening – room filled with candles, in Japan, go on –

JERRY. so then at a certain point someone
steps forward and begins to tell a story,
a ghost story, and at the end of the story
the uh teller extinguishes the candle –
and then another person steps forward
and tells another story, and tries to make their story
even scarier than the last, and when they're done,
they extinguish another candle, and –

SYLVIA. for every candle?/ Jesus sounds like torture

JERRY. /uh-huh

LINDA. fifty/ candles!

JERRY. oh it goes on for hours really,
until there's just one candle left,
and then the last person tries to tell
the scariest story of the night,
and once it's told, the last candle gets blown out,
and then everyone's just left in total darkness.

LINDA. ...well so what was the last story?

JERRY. uhhh/hhhh –

SYLVIA. better have been worth it

JERRY. you know I don't remember

SYLVIA. well there you go

JERRY. it's on the tip of my brain – this is going to/ drive me crazy

LINDA. you'll remember and you'll tell/ us and –

JERRY. *(The wine is uncorked;* **JERRY,** *offering.)* there we go – Hilda, may I–?

HILDA. oh alright –

LINDA. *(Adjusts herself.)* I would like to raise a little toast to my dear dear cousin Jerry – my American cousin – oh I remember when I first met little Jerry so many years ago – you were this tall – this tall –! And now –ha ha – you're my savior

JERRY. naw –

LINDA. saved me from being carted off back to England, and for that I'll be forever grateful.

JERRY. No I'm just happy that I could finally be useful to someone in this world

LINDA. more than useful, more than –

SYLVIA. To Linda.

LINDA. Oh!

SYLVIA. right? – To Linda,
who I consider both a friend –
a very close friend – a friend I wish I saw more of
but I know she's in demand so I'll take what I can get –
And, to the Linda who I consider a
mentor, um,
because you have – you've taught me so much
about life, and priorities,
and – especially after my divorce – um
helping me through a really hard time,
and I will never forget that.
So thank you.
And I'm happy you're here –

JERRY. yes. To Linda.
To Linda – yay – cheers/ cheers –

HILDA. cheers

SYLVIA. Jerry –cheers –

LINDA. cheers.

(Full beat to drink.)

...oh this is very good, Sylvia

JERRY. /oh yeah –

SYLVIA. well unfortunately I'm worried now I didn't buy enough wine –

JERRY. /naw we're fine –

SYLVIA. *(To* **LINDA.***)* didn't know that you'd be bringing your uh friend, I didn't/ – just feel a little embarrassed that I –

LINDA. it's fine – you're a wonderful host – thank you for –

JERRY. So Linda –

LINDA. /yes

JERRY. how does it feel being an American

LINDA. well I'm not –

JERRY. one step closer –

LINDA. honestly...?
It feels fucking wonderful – it does –
no really, I love America.
I love this country. I do.
Much prefer it to dreary England,
dreary England with its dreary weather,
and dreary people,

dreary history,
always looking back – I'll tell you what I so love about
all of you – in America,
you look forward.
In America you all really believe – deep down –
you believe that you can be whatever
you want to be, and that just strikes me as
the most wonderful thing –

well and you know this is the birthplace
of what I do – all of the great spiritualists/ –
all Americans.

JERRY. really, huh.

LINDA. And I won't lie,
I'm treated better in America – I'm
better at my job in /America – seriously –

JERRY. it's the accent,/ isn't it

LINDA. It is – it is! I have such authority here
that I didn't have there.
There I always had to work so hard at it, but here – here
I open my mouth and everyone listens. I'm wise! –
like an old sage from another land –

SYLVIA. Well you better like it here, because
you don't really have another option –

LINDA. /ha ha ha! –

JERRY. Sylvia!

SYLVIA. What!

LINDA. You're being naughty, Sylvia – Don't make me bend you over

SYLVIA. yes please

LINDA. no, but it is true – they did run me out of the country

JERRY. well... I wouldn't/ put it that way

LINDA. criminal charges pending – no
other way to put it – ha ha!
No, what I blame is the EU – the fucking – excuse me –
the fucking European Union – what with all of their
rules – their little rules about
what a medium can and can't do –
regulations, mandatory disclaimers –

well I'm not going to do it.
It ruins the experience to start off a reading by saying
I'm not real. I'm just entertainment. I have no powers –
It ruins the mood is/ what it –

JERRY. is there more wine?

SYLVIA. What do you/ want?

JERRY. No no no, you sit, I'll/ get it

SYLVIA. but what do/ you – ?

JERRY. Linda – ?

LINDA. white/ thank you

SYLVIA. down the stairs, to the left, in the second fridge –

JERRY. the second

SYLVIA. smaller –

JERRY. yep.

(**JERRY** *exits.*)

SYLVIA. ...So how did you manage to get your visa – ?

LINDA. How?

SYLVIA. – last time I talked to you – they had
denied your application – In fact,
didn't you call me because you thought you
were going to need some money – ?

LINDA. yes,/ yes well –

SYLVIA. and then I never heard anything else, and –

LINDA. they did deny it at first –

SYLVIA. /why?

LINDA. because apparently the occupation of
"psychic" sounds not very legitimate
to the people who grant visas – and it's so hard

to talk about/ what I do –

SYLVIA. so did you – ?

LINDA. no, Jerry sorted it/ out –

> (**JERRY** *re-enters with another bottle of wine.*)

JERRY. what did I sort out –

LINDA. the visa –

SYLVIA. how?

JERRY. I made some calls and –

LINDA. you know he's got special/ connections because of his work with the –

JERRY. it's nothing all that interesting

LINDA. and then he got me a legitimate job working with one of his/ people, on one of his –

JERRY. Linda Linda /Linda Linda

LINDA. oh well now shit! – was I not supposed to talk/ about that

JERRY. I'd prefer you didn't

LINDA. oh but can't I just tell them, Jerry. Please can I – they won't tell anyone – you won't/ tell anyone

SYLVIA. tell what?

JERRY. Okay, let's just – you know – none of this leaves this room –

SYLVIA. *oh*

JERRY. not because anything "illegal" is happening, or – just – see now we're making it worse by being mysterious/ about it

LINDA. you were the one being/ mysterious

JERRY. No – it's just that – so one of my clients is this guy who is –

SYLVIA. running for office –?

JERRY. running for office who has been
struggling – who is – he's a terrific guy –
he just, for whatever reason, didn't
have the ability to really
grab people –

LINDA. that's an understatement –

JERRY. And I was thinking about it one night and it just sorta hit me that – I mean if you look at it from the right angle – that's what Linda does – she grabs people's minds – people she's never met before, somehow she just manages to work her way in there, and people end up really trusting her – for, no apparent reason – and if he could do that, well – And then I remembered your issue with the visa and thought my problem could solve your problem and vice versa – so what's there to/ lose –

SYLVIA. Who is it –?

LINDA. Sylvia, he can't tell you that

JERRY. someone in one of the fifty states/ – ha ha ha ha

SYLVIA. would I know the person –?

LINDA. stop asking questions – it's making Jerry/ uncomfortable –

SYLVIA. okay but so you help this guy – what, how/ – you

LINDA. when I watched 'im, watched 'im talkin' to people,
an' I saw how he was
just no good at it – so I worked with him,
taught him little things he could do,
body language, non-verbal cues, ways of
inflecting his voice
to help people have an easier time agreeing with him –

JERRY. /yeah that stuff is great

LINDA. but mainly it was that he didn't understand his
role – didn't understand
what people needed from him – kind of
missed the whole point/ of it –

SYLVIA. which is what – what's/ the –

LINDA. the point of it is – well, when people come to me, they come to me knowin' already what they think. They know what they're lookin' to hear – an' my job is to work <u>with</u> them – to hear what inklin' they got in their head – say it back to them, help make it real. An' sometimes what they've got in their head isn't very nice, might even be painful – might be they suspect their husband cheated on 'em or their brother killed himself. You might think, *just tell 'em it was an accident*, but no – you've got to voice what they know inside, say, *yes, he was sufferin'*, but then you can say, *he knows you did everything you could and he loves you so much.*

Cuz we actually want to – need to hear
that the monster's waitin' just round the corner –
that the world is comin' to an end,
and tellin' them that there's nothing to fear
only makes them feel they've gone mental – ha ha –
even if they/ are a little –

JERRY. yeah, that's true – no/ it definitely –

LINDA. so I say to Jerry's fellow – I tell 'im, *You need to figure out what these people are scared of – An' don't tell them it's not real – you've to let them know you see it too –* so then you can say, *hey, I can make that scary thing go away, I can kill the monster but only if you let me, only if you put me in charge –*

SYLVIA. You know who did that, don't you.

LINDA. Who?

SYLVIA. Hitler.

LINDA. Oh...

SYLVIA. he did, he hired a popular mind reader of the time –

JERRY. /what!?! – noooo –

SYLVIA. it's true

LINDA. /oh for the love of –

SYLVIA. Hitler hired a mind reader because he saw that the guy was so good at controlling crowds, manipulating their minds –

JERRY. /no one's manipulating anyone –

SYLVIA. in his act he had these very commanding hand gestures and Hitler was impressed with all of that – It's where Hitler got all his hand gestures from – !

LINDA. 's the one thing I find irritating about you Americans –

SYLVIA. /what

LINDA. – your obsession with Hitler

SYLVIA. /I'm just saying that –

LINDA. you are all obsessed – when in doubt "Hitler" – whenever you want to prove your point you just shout out "Hitler" – you love it, gets you worked up – oh I'm talking about Hitler,/ ooo, gettin' all excited talkin' about Nazis –

SYLVIA. no, that's not true, oh come on –

JERRY. I just want to be clear, everyone: the person that Linda and I are working with is not Hitler – he is not – /let's just be clear –

LINDA. oh no no no, he's very nice, very

sweet fellow – not even close to Hitler – isn't that funny:
you could not pick a more
un-Hitler kind of person –
and the funny thing is, that's sort of his problem.

JERRY. right /right right – ha ha

LINDA. 'f you ask me he could stand to have a
little more of – not – not in the
killing-of-innocent people/ sort of way –
of course – ha ha –

JERRY. oh no no no no no no

SYLVIA. ...

LINDA. what.

What, you have a look on your face, you have a –

SYLVIA. nothing

I don't know.

Just isn't it a little dishonest, isn't it a little –

LINDA. /in what way dishonest?

SYLVIA. I don't want to use the word manipulative –

LINDA. well you just/ did, you just did

JERRY. but it's not really –

SYLVIA. it's just kind of depressing though, isn't it?

JERRY. See, this is exactly why we don't talk about this, Linda

LINDA. /I know, I know

SYLVIA. How do you even feel about this candidate –?

LINDA. I told you/ I like him

SYLVIA. and you support his ideas

LINDA. he has very good ideas

SYLVIA. like what, for example –?

LINDA. I'm not going to sit here and – you'd vote for him. He's in that party that you vote for –

SYLVIA. okay, well/ I mean, that at least is a good thing, I guess, but –

LINDA. I mean Jerry and I wouldn't be helping out one of those other ones –

SYLVIA. but still –

LINDA. but/ still what?

SYLVIA. just sort of feels like it opens the door to something –

LINDA. /opening a door to what?

SYLVIA. you know whatever tricks/ Linda's teaching him – it's kind of like "mind control" isn't it?

LINDA. tricks – what tricks – ?

JERRY. I mean, I get it Sylvia – we all want to think
that the best idea wins,
but I'm sorry to say that's just not how it works.
Because no matter how good or smart your ideas are,
the bad ones – the bad ideas, the bad voices –
those are always going to be louder,
well, because honestly they're just more interesting.
And the scary voices – oh the scary ones, they're
like a car wreck –
you can't help but stare at the wreckage.
And so – I'm sorry – but in light of all of that
we have to do whatever we can
to make the good – albeit boring – voices louder –
that's all – It's called being persuasive.

SYLVIA. …Well okay, I–

LINDA. Jerry can I have some more of that –

/thank you.

JERRY. So, Sylvia. Linda was telling me that you've been traveling the world this past month.

SYLVIA. Yes, I have been–

JERRY. Where did you go – ?

SYLVIA. it was amazing it was amazing –

I was in Norway for two weeks,
and Norway – none of you have/ been, right – ?

JERRY. no, I haven't

HILDA. no

SYLVIA. it's really, amazing – it's a country
where I think they got a lot of things really right,
and where the level of equality,
and their sense of compassionate justice
is really something – there's a lot we could
learn from them –

JERRY. /yeah wow

SYLVIA. I mean could go on about the Norwegian prison system

for hours...

but I won't – ha ha! – but um...

then I made a brief stop in Spain

JERRY. in –

SYLVIA. Barcelona

JERRY. oh nice –

SYLVIA. just a couple of days, visited a friend, did a little shopping, and–

but the highlight of the trip was

when I was in Denmark and
I met this woman, and I mean, she was
the most amazing woman –
she was sixty three, she swam a mile every day –
her arms were – you wouldn't believe it,
I mean just incredible, and she lives in this
shack on the edge of the forest,
owns almost nothing, like the bare minimum of what
you need to survive,
and guess how much she's worth –?

JERRY. hmmmmm –

SYLVIA. one hundred and seventy million –

JERRY. /oh

SYLVIA. easily – most of it family money, you know –
but she only lives off of like
a thousand dollars a year, if that,
and anything she doesn't need to
keep a roof over her head
and food on the table, she gives away.
All of it. Sends it off to other parts of the world where
people have nothing, where children are
starving, where there's terrible suffering –
And every day we would spend hours talking,
and she told me – she was like it's very simple:
she believed that any money that
isn't spent on the absolute necessities of survival
is money that has a child's blood on it.

And I have to say I found it very difficult to argue with/ that

JERRY. I could argue with that

LINDA. so could I –

SYLVIA. I don't know I don't know – really got me to thinking

JERRY. of living in a shack?

SYLVIA. I am strongly considering

JERRY. /nooooo

SYLVIA. end of next year, I really think I might
make a big life change,
I might move into a more modest place
and live on a lot less than I live on now – I mean
this is a – what – two hundred dollar wine glass?
There are two dollar wine glasses that'll
do the job just fine,
and the difference is money that could feed a starving
child in some place like South Sudan.

JERRY. well –

LINDA. no, now this is the other thing that
really irritates me about you Americans:
there's the Hitler thing,
and then there's this guilt you all seem to have –

SYLVIA. /guilt?

LINDA. yes, guilt for all of your success, and
for having /done so well –

JERRY. it's not untrue –

LINDA. of course it's true – and I see it – see this guilt
sneaking into your country, its politics –
it's very insidious – and all because, for some reason,
you're not okay getting everything you want –
so you beat yourself up,

self-flagellation

SYLVIA. wanting to help someone isn't a bad thing –

JERRY. no, of/ course not

LINDA. no, this goes far beyond that – I can hear in your
voice this –

SYLVIA. you're just worried that if I give away all my money there won't be any left for you

LINDA. when have I ever asked you for money

SYLVIA. you don't so much ask as/ you imply –

LINDA. imply, oh / I imply do I

SYLVIA. you put me in a position where I'm feeling guilty, like/ I'm abandoning you if I don't –

LINDA. don't blame me for your feelings –
your feelings are your feelings.
Please Sylvia, do NOT give me any more of your money –
I won't accept it, alright –?

do what you want, I don't/ care

JERRY. if I can just weigh in –

LINDA. /please do

JERRY. here's the thing: just looking at the facts,
looking at the numbers,
on the whole everything is getting better –
across the board –
infant mortality, education, hunger – so that
the kind of suffering that you're talking about
has decreased so rapidly in just even the past fifty years –

SYLVIA. but it still exists

JERRY. but it's getting better
and not because people such as yourself
have deprived themselves and gone the "martyr route"'–

SYLVIA. not talking about being a martyr/ – I'm just –

JERRY. well, I mean, when/ you talk about –

SYLVIA. I just mean that I could give more

JERRY. maybe.

But even that – even throwing money that

you can afford to throw
at the problem – even that – I mean there's the argument –
and I have this book you should read
I can send you a copy – that the money
you're putting out there can actually
make the problems worse –
destabilizing local economies, feeding corruption, hell,
that two dollar wine glass – if you look at
how that's made –
that alone probably causes more
suffering/ in the world than the
one hundred and ninety eight dollar fixes –

SYLVIA. okay okay forget the wine glass

JERRY. truth is, the fact that things have gotten better
is due to all these very hard to understand,
very complicated, almost invisible movements
in the economy, in the world –
all of it way beyond anything one person can/ control –

SYLVIA. even a food bank, Jerry – you're saying even a food bank is –

JERRY. oh my God, food banks are the worst! –

SYLVIA. /how –?!?

JERRY. food banks hurt local farmers and they
hurt the people who sell food –
No I'm sorry I tend to think that by-and-large
most charities are really only there
to make the people giving the money feel
better about themselves –
and when you consider the fact that a lot of that money
can make things worse –
well, a lot of charity, if you really think about it,
is actually pretty selfish

SYLVIA. that's crazy

JERRY. hey, just do a little reading –

SYLVIA. no, I'm sure I could go and read
whatever book it is you're going to send me
and I'm sure it says exactly what you're saying
with graphs and numbers and – but I'm
sure I could also find plenty of things to read
with different graphs and numbers
that say the opposite –

JERRY. I'm telling you which one is right

SYLVIA. and why would I believe you?

JERRY. I don't know, Sylvia – why do you believe anything?

SYLVIA. I don't know, Jerry – you're so smart – you tell me.

JERRY. Honestly, I just think it comes out of a
need to feel important –
what you're believing here
sort of puts you at the center of everything,
and ignores reality, in favor making you
feel/ like you're the –

SYLVIA. I just think it's interesting how you cultivated a world view that requires the least possible sacrifice from you

LINDA. Sylvia…

I'm getting an awful lot of negative energy from you tonight

SYLVIA. what does that mean

LINDA. it means you're being a real cunt.
Stop it. Alright?

SYLVIA. …

LINDA. Or if you've got something on your mind that you'd like to say to me, then just spit it out, because –

SYLVIA. I think you take advantage of people.

LINDA. Alright.

How –

SYLVIA. all sorts of ways

LINDA. be specific

SYLVIA. with what you do–

LINDA. what I do, meaning – what do you mean "what I do"

SYLVIA. you know –

LINDA. my work as a medium?

SYLVIA. It's just all of this meddling – meddling, meddling with people's minds –

LINDA. what meddling! – what/ is she talking about?

JERRY. naw I'm just gonna stay out of this –

SYLVIA. no, I do – I do I think that you're
taking advantage –
when people are coming to you
at the worst times of their lives –
and you take their money and tell them lies –
and yeah you tell them lies to make them feel better,
and maybe it does, but you're still lying to people –
and I've been thinking about this for awhile now, and
I think what you do does a lot of harm –

LINDA. Harm? Sylvia, you have no idea what you're talking about – why – you go take some little pudgy girl/ with

SYLVIA. yes yes with the greasy hair and
the pimples on her face
and tears in her eyes and the dead father
who loves her very much, but what if –
what if, actually, her father didn't love her,

and what if he treated her badly – you don't know –
and you've gone and made her think that
her horrible childhood wasn't so horrible.
And maybe she <u>needs</u> to know that
actually he didn't love her and that that was
the reality, and to let her tell herself
that something was something that it wasn't –
doesn't that at certain point
just gradually sort of take you away from yourself
and away from what you see?

LINDA. But what that is, is that girl seeing through me
what she needs to see,
and far be it from me to tell her
that she's not seeing what she needs to see –
that – that would be cruel…hurtful –

SYLVIA. how do you know that – how can you know/ for sure that –

LINDA. Why! – I don't even properly know
what I'm doing when I'm doing what I'm doing –
it's something that happens through me

SYLVIA. but you know, you/ know that it's not –

LINDA. I'm telling you, I know nothing.
I claim to know nothing
which probably makes me the most
honest person in this room.

SYLVIA. …

LINDA. But now let's talk about you, Sylvia.
You come at me, accusing me of
taking advantage of people,
but you don't <u>really</u> believe that, do you.
No, what you're really trying to say to me
is that you think I take advantage of <u>you</u>.
Isn't that right?

SYLVIA. / Yeah, well...

LINDA. But have you ever stopped to think
about the ways in which,
actually, you take advantage of me?
Do you ever stop to think about all of the late night calls,
all of the advice you're always asking for,
all of the emotional support that you need,
and how draining it must be to someone like me,
who is always trying to give so much to so many people.
Do you ever think about me and how I'm feeling –
do you even care?

Seriously Sylvia, sometimes I'm surprised by your total lack of self-awareness.

(SYLVIA walks off.)

JERRY. ...

HILDA. ...

LINDA. I do find it very interesting how it's
the so-called "victimized"
who are often the victimizers.

(Offstage, SYLVIA smashes a wine glass.)

Well, there goes two hundred dollars.

JERRY. ...

LINDA. ...alright alright, I'll go after her.

(JERRY and HILDA, alone.)

JERRY. A little drama.
A little dinner and a show, right? – ha ha ha...

HILDA. ...yeah.

JERRY. ...

HILDA. ...

JERRY. How're ya' holdin' up there – can I get you anything – ?

HILDA. oh, no I'm fine

JERRY. great.

HILDA. ...

JERRY. "Hilda".

What kind of name is that?

HILDA. Northern, of some kind.

JERRY. Right.

HILDA. *(Smiles.)* ...

JERRY. You don't say much do you.

HILDA. Oh, I like to listen.

JERRY. You do. Yes. I can tell.
No, I like that about you, that you listen.

HILDA. *(Smiles.)* Thanks.

JERRY. Do you want any more –?

HILDA. okay

(Pours her some more wine.)

thanks.

JERRY. So what it is it that you hear?

HILDA. Oh, I don't know – tonight, you mean?

JERRY. Sure.

HILDA. Oh. People. Talking. Having fun.
Having fun telling each other stories.
Having fun drinking.

JERRY. Yeah.

Yeah, that's about it.
Plus a little desperation

HILDA. ha ha – yeah, maybe

JERRY. yeah – ?

HILDA. oh I don't know.

JERRY. we're all a lonely lot, aren't we.

HILDA. I suppose – what do you think they're doing in there?

JERRY. Oh who knows.
You know Linda. She and Sylvia,
they're always doing this dance.

HILDA. ...dance?

JERRY. Oh you know –
Hey – you know
we've hung out a little at Linda's get togethers,
but really, I feel like I know next to nothing about you.

HILDA. oh there's nothing to know

JERRY. I'm sure that's not true

HILDA. oh it is

JERRY. what is it that you do for work.

HILDA. Nothing special. I answer phones.
For a store.

JERRY. Oh

HILDA. yeah. See?
Not so interesting is it

JERRY. no

HILDA. probably sorry you asked

JERRY. no, not at all, no no,
no – I have to admit.

I'd been asking Linda about you.
Asking her all sorts of – because you are kind of quiet, kind of – so I ask her...
I ask her, hey, what's Hilda into.
What's she all about.
What's she doing with you and not me – ha ha ha – just kidding, just – no she uh...

She describes you as a very curious person.

HILDA. Oh that's nice

JERRY. yeah, she was um – I guess she was sort of kidding, joking, she was "Hilda – why is she so..."

HILDA. What

JERRY. no she enjoys you, she does, she really –

enjoys spending time with you, having you around – and I mean, you know her health hasn't been great lately –

HILDA. with the –

JERRY. yeah, it's gotten worse,
so it certainly helps to have someone
around, to look after –

HILDA. uh huh.

JERRY. And of course, she does love an audience,
loves having someone who will listen to her go on –
and you do – you listen – and you actually seem to like it

HILDA. ...

JERRY. and I know you're really into the work she does,
and I think she appreciates that you're into it... I also –
I also think she maybe thinks you're
a little...sometimes...

well she's never put it this way, but maybe a little too...

into it – in a way that I think...

– I mean, *I* don't think it's weird,
I think it's really special to find someone
still capable of uh –
who has such an open mind

HILDA. ...uh-huh

JERRY. she says you tell these adorable stories about growing up, and your grandmother

HILDA. oh she told you about that?

JERRY. Just in passing. Just...

HILDA. ...

JERRY. oh.

I just remembered it –

HILDA. ...

JERRY. the scariest story in Japan...the one I was trying to remember earlier, but couldn't, but –

You want to hear it?

HILDA. ...okay

JERRY. now how exactly did it go?

uhhhhh

there's a man.
And this man – he's a...terrible –
just a terrible, violent, angry human.
Nasty.

And he's married to this woman.
And they've been married for years,
and over the years, you know his wife sort of...
gradually changed –

you know, like people do, she...
she just sort of –
And the husband, he has these scissors,
this pair of really sharp scissors

>*(A shriek offstage!)*

>*(Followed by laughter.)*

>*(**LINDA** and **SYLVIA** re-enter, **LINDA**'s wearing a new dress.)*

ladies ladies ladies

LINDA. Look at me –!!!
look at this dress – this wonderful dress Sylvia got me.
Does it look fetching? Ha ha –

JERRY. oh wow/ yeah

SYLVIA. bought it for her when I was in Barcelona

JERRY. very nice

LINDA. isn't it?

JERRY. hey hey hey I remembered the scariest story in Japan –

LINDA. oh what is it

JERRY. so there's his man, and he's just this/ horrible –

SYLVIA. no, don't – I can't, it's too close to bedtime, and I can tell we're winding down for the night and/I can't no, please, no –

LINDA. I want to hear it

SYLVIA. no, seriously, that's the kind of thing that when I'm in bed tonight and the lights are turned out – that's the kind of thing that's going to sneak back into my head –

JERRY. okay alright

LINDA. /boo

SYLVIA. no I'm just too susceptible – it's too easy for me to get a thought in my head that sort of roots itself in there –

JERRY. right, yeah, no I know what you mean –

SYLVIA. hey – is there any more of that – hey, you – Heidi?

JERRY. Hilda

SYLVIA. huh – ?

JERRY. Hilda

SYLVIA. what did I say

JERRY. Heidi

SYLVIA. what did you say

JERRY. Hilda

HILDA. I have a story.

LINDA. ooo, Hilda tells the most interesting stories –

SYLVIA. /oh really

JERRY. is this one of the ones about your grandmother?

HILDA. ...no this one is about my mother –
about the last time I ever saw her

LINDA. oh I don't know any about your mother –

HILDA. I know.

So, the last time I ever saw my mother –
was last Christmas.

Um.

I hadn't been to visit in awhile – hadn't
been around much you know –
But it was Christmas, and Christmas that's what you do.
You pay a little visit.

You put in a little time.
You bring a gift, you drop it off,
you sit on the couch, you talk for about a half an hour,
and then you say, okay, well, nice to see you,
I have to go now, I have this thing I have to do – You've put in your time,
you're free to go.

But this time when I visited her...
She just looked bad.
She had this massive bruise down the side of her face.

And it was just really bad.

And...

At first I just said nothing.

I just stared at her...

but eventually I said something I don't remember what – probably Merry Christmas,
because, well that's what you do and

and then I sort of asked what happened to her face

and she said she fell

and I asked "when"

and she said she didn't remember.

And so that was
probably the first concerning thing of that afternoon.

And then inside the house,
the place was a mess.
Trash just everywhere
And the kitchen was like something out of a nightmare,

just horrible,
dirty and
and and there were these cans, open cans of
green beans and corn and
and and
a cluster of the silverfish by the sink faucet,

and she seemed to be unaware of how disgusting it was.
She would – I actually saw her do this – she'd
pick up a spoon and
she'd pick at the stuff in the cans –
have a little corn or –
the stuff was rotten, or it must've been,
it had been sitting there for days, I'm sure.

It was all so completely shocking.
The kind of shocking that just makes you
mad at the person – mad at the person with the
bruised up face – which I know sounds just terrible
and maybe it is – but you look at that
person and Jesus fucking Christ – get yourself together
Life isn't *that* hard, is it?

And then when it's your mother –
well that only intensifies the feeling of disgust because
really what you're thinking is – is that going to be me?
Am I going to someday completely lose
all sense of dignity?

So I really wasn't sure what to do. About my mother.
I mean you do what you can:
I did what cleaning I could, barely made a dent though –
what was I supposed to do move in with her,
take care of her?
but that's not a real option, I mean,
it's not like I'm a professional care taker.
Then do you hire someone? –

Well who has money for that –? She doesn't.
I don't.

But then I thought to myself, you know there
are other options,
public options, facilities, care-taking facilities –
not the type of thing she would have wanted per se,
not the type of thing she would ever agree to.
No, she would never want to leave her home.

But you know…there are scenarios in which
it would be out of anyone's control,
like, if, for example –

Like if a neighbor saw her
walking around outside with her face like it was,
all bruised like it was – if a neighbor saw that, then
a neighbor would likely call Health and Human Services
and they would send someone to check on her,
and if that person from Health and Human Services
saw the house the way it was,
and her face the way it was,
they would have no choice – they would be
legally obligated to take her in.

And so…

I decided that I would place a call,
tell them that I was her neighbor,
and tell them that I saw her,
out walking in the yard,
and that she seemed not well and that
her face was bruised.

And after I made the call,
I just waited.

Waited a week.

But I heard nothing.

So I called back.
Health and Human Services.
I got the case worker that I'd spoken with earlier,
and I knew that they wouldn't be able to say much to me
on account of they thought I was just the "neighbor,"
but they did say that
they thought everything would be fine.

And I said, s*o she's staying?*

And they told me that an examiner or something went,
and yes, the house was messy,
but they got to talk for a bit to her family
and since she had family around
they weren't too worried
and that's all they could really say,
and –
I mean, family?

Who was there? – I wasn't there –

and I said real casual like it was nothing,
Oh so her family was at the house.

And the case worker said yes,
and thanked me for my concern,
and that was it.

…

Weird, right?

But I thought to myself *oh maybe there was some friend of hers around*
but she doesn't have any friends.

And so I called my mother.

She says hello.
I say hello back.

I ask how she's doing.

She says, *oh just fine.*

And I'm trying to think,
so how do I ask what I want to ask?

Of course I don't want her to know that I
called the Health and Human Services on her,
and so –
so I say

*Hey mom, I got a call from Health and Human Services
and they said they had to pay you a visit. What's that
about? Is that true?*

And she said her neighbor had called them on her,
and that she was really upset about
her neighbor doing that
and that she talked to the neighbor and the neighbor
denied doing anything, calling, and so on –

and I said *oh well, I just wanted to
make sure everything was okay,
because that call got me worried.*

And she said, *No, there's nothing to worry about.*

...

And then I said,
I told her that there was just one more thing though
that I wanted to ask her about.
I said that the case worker said that when they visited

that there was
some "family"
there,
and that that sounded odd
and I asked my mother
if that's true.
Was there somebody else there with her when
the Health and Human such and such person was
paying the visit,
and
she said
yes.

And I asked,

Who? Who exactly was there with her.

And there was silence.

And then very slowly she said

Would you like to talk to them?

…

And I said
Sure.

And I could hear her put down the phone.

And it took a little while.
I could hear very faint
murmuring in the background,
it wasn't clear, it was
something like voices –

and after a little bit
I hear the phone pick up

and

I said, *hello?*

And there was silence.

And then a voice

on the other end –

I don't know if it was a man or a woman I couldn't tell –
I couldn't tell the age –

but the person said

I know you.

That's what the person said to me –
the person said to me:

I know you.

...

And I asked, *Okay, and who are you?*

And the voice said again
exactly the same way:
I know you.

And I asked again, *who is this?*
Who are you? Are you a friend of my mother's?

No answer.

And I said,
I'm going to call the police. Alright?
I'm calling the police.

And still no response.

And I said, *Put my mother back on the phone.*

And the voice said,

We're in the other place now.

...

And it said again.

*We're in the
other place now.*

And then the phone hung up.
And I called back,
and it was disconnected
or something.

I called the police.

They went to the house.

They called me back.

They said there was nobody in the house.

...

They put out a missing person's something-or-rather.
They did a search. They did all the things they do –
They put up posters in her neighborhood,
and local news alert and...

So.

Nothing.

Never turned up.

And that was almost a year ago.

(Silence in the room.)

(Just silence.)

(No one really knows what to say.)

JERRY. wow Hilda.
um.
wow...

    (...And more silence.)

    *(**HILDA**'s phone rings, loud, startling everyone.)*

    (Shriek, laughter, tension broken.)

HILDA. Sorry, that's my phone.

LINDA. Oh that nearly gave us all a heart attack

JERRY. that was – ha ha – yes, that was quite a startle/ there. Perfect timing

SYLVIA. scared the living shit out of me.

HILDA. ...

LINDA. ...

    *(To **SYLVIA**.)*

Do you want to help me finish this –?

SYLVIA. oh like you have to ask...

    *(**HILDA**'s is starring at her phone.)*

JERRY. ...Hilda?

You alright?

HILDA. ...

LINDA. Hilda –

HILDA. *(Holding out the phone as "evidence.")* that call.
That call was from my mother's house.

LINDA. ...

JERRY. ...huh.

You sure?

HILDA. *(Nods "yes.")* ...

JERRY. Huh

LINDA. well now isn't that odd –

JERRY. And does anyone live there now?

HILDA. No.
No.

SYLVIA. So creepy –

JERRY. well...

LINDA. I think you should just give it a call back. See what happens...

HILDA. ...

JERRY. You don't have to –

HILDA. okay.

> (**HILDA** *dials, on speaker phone, holding it out so everyone can bear witness...*)
>
> *(...)*
>
> *(Sound of a disconnected line.)*
>
> (**PHONE**: *I'm sorry but this line has been disconnected.*)
>
> (**HILDA** *hangs up.*)

JERRY. ...You know it was probably some sort of

random phone glitch,
or – I mean I don't know much about
phones, phone numbers, how they – but there's probably
some explanation for – for <u>all</u> of this
that makes total sense, that's completely ordinary and
would never occur to us because of a piece of information
we don't have or a –

> (**PHONE** *rings again.*)

HILDA. ...

> (**PHONE** *rings.*)

JERRY. ...

> (**PHONE** *rings.*)

HILDA. It's her.

> (**PHONE** *rings.*)

JERRY. Do you want to answer it?

> (**PHONE** *rings.*)

HILDA. ...alright.

> (*Presses "answer".*)

PHONE. ...

HILDA. ...

PHONE. ...

HILDA. Hello...?

> (*Silence as everyone stares at the phone –*)
>
> (*Lights cut to black...*)

AFTER THE PARTY

HILDA. ...and I thought I could hear something, like a voice,
on the other end of the line,

and Jerry agreed that he heard something too,
and Sylvia, she looked like she might start crying,
like she was actually really scared.

But Linda...

Linda acted like nothing had happened
and said she was done for the night
and told me to drive her home.

> *(A single red lightbulb slowly fades up. It dimly lights the stage.)*

In the car,
Linda wouldn't talk to me.

> *(Silence.)*

LINDA. ...

HILDA. Linda?

LINDA. ...

HILDA. Why aren't you saying anything.

LINDA. ...

HILDA. ...

LINDA. ...

HILDA. ...Linda –?

LINDA. I'm thinking.

HILDA. ...About what.

LINDA. I think that when you
drop me off at my flat tonight,
I'd like to be alone.

And you should go back to your home,
and I think
we should not visit with each other
for awhile.

HILDA. um...

why do you say that...?

LINDA. ...we've lost ourselves a little,
haven't we, Hilda

HILDA. ...I don't know what that means

LINDA. ...

HILDA. ...are you mad at me about tonight?

LINDA. Well it was a bit much, don't you think

HILDA. ...what was

LINDA. your little story.
You were wantin' a bit of attention,
and you got it. Are you happy?

HILDA. That was real. That was a true story.

...But no matter what I said,
Linda didn't seem to believe me.

I wanted her to know that what happened
really happened

I wanted her to know that
I've seen things,
I've experienced things

that are more than just tricks,

more than just thoughts in your head –

and so

when we we got to the right turn that would
take us to where Linda lived
...I took the left turn –

LINDA. Hilda.

HILDA. the left turn that would take us to my mother's house.

LINDA. Hilda – where are you taking me

HILDA. and Linda – she did, she got very mad at me,
she demanded to know where I was taking her,
demanded that I turn around –
She told me she'd never talk to me again if I didn't
take her home immediately,
but I kept on driving until...

We're here.

LINDA. ...

HILDA. So, are you coming inside with me?

LINDA. ...No, Hilda.
I'm not

HILDA. come inside with me,
and I promise I'll take you home if you –

LINDA. Hilda, it's late.

And I'm not feeling well.

HILDA. Please,
please come with me

I want to know what's in there.

And I want you to know too.

LINDA. *(Very quiet.)* ...

...

...alright, Hilda.

HILDA. It was very very late at night,

and because the doors were locked
and the house was all boarded up,
I had to go around to the back of the house
and break a window just to get in.

We climbed through the window –
there wasn't any power on in the house, so we
had to feel our way around.

This is it, I said.
This is the house I grew up in.

Hello?

Is anybody here?

I decided we should have a look around –
I took Linda by the hand,
I walked her from room to room...

I said,

this is the kitchen,
and this is the room where we'd eat our meals.

And through that little door you can
go out to the backyard.
It's not much, just a narrow patch of dirt.

Here's the extra room where my

grandmother stayed when she lived with us.

And this is my bedroom –

I remember walking in here once,
not long after my grandmother had died,
and saw my mother curled up on the floor.
She was crying. She thought she had a demon in her(?),
and she said *get it out of me, get it out, you're my daughter and you have to fix me.*
And so I got down on the floor with her,
and she grabbed onto my wrist, I remember that, like
this, real tight, I remember,
and she had me put my fingers in her mouth, dig around,
see if I could
help pull whatever it was out of her.
And I sort of felt like I felt something soft...
but I don't know...

And this – this is
my mother's room.

The door is closed.
That's odd.

I'm sort of scared to open it.
Should I open it?

I'm going to open it.

...I opened the door.

And

we walked in

...and there was...

Nothing.

Nothing in my mother's room.

Nothing anywhere.

...It was just an empty house.

LINDA. Hilda...

have you seen what you wanted to see..?

can we go now

HILDA. mm hm

LINDA. ...

HILDA. ...

> *(In the darkness we can hear the faint sound of* **HILDA** *crying.)*

LINDA. ...you a'right

HILDA. mm-hm

LINDA. ...

HILDA. ...

LINDA. ...why don't you

...call her

call your mother

HILDA. ...

LINDA. I think you should call your mother
like how you'd call your gran
back when you were a child
all alone
in your bedroom...

I think you should talk to her...

HILDA. ...

LINDA. you'll feel better

HILDA. no it's not real

LINDA. but maybe it is,
and maybe I can't do it for real,
but you can.

HILDA. I've never done it with anyone watching.

LINDA. I won't say a word.

HILDA. ...

LINDA. I could step outside

HILDA. no.

um...

LINDA. would you like me to make it so you can't see me

HILDA. ...okay

LINDA. see that sheet on the bed.
Hand it to me...

(**HILDA** *hands* **LINDA** *a sheet.*)

(**LINDA** *puts it over her head.*)

like I'm not even here.

HILDA. ...

LINDA. ...

HILDA. Go stand over there

LINDA. over there

HILDA. yes.

(**LINDA** *gets up, goes over the back wall.*)

HILDA. ...

LINDA. alright..?

HILDA. turn around..?

> *(LINDA does so.)*

mm-hm...

Alright.

shhhhhhhhh

now how does this go...

I breathe.

I breathe,

and I let my eyes go soft.

Focus on the light, the little bit of light there.

Focus on the dark around the light

because the senses need to be soft,

the outside senses – soft,

the inside senses – also soft,

but the inside senses by themself they get sharp

very sharp

and I hum
just to myself
a single tone

> *(She starts giggling a little – a little tipsy? But then very serious.)*

okay.

hello?

mom

are you here?

I feel something

I think it's you

I hope you're not mad at me.

I'm sorry...that

I didn't take better care of you

that I couldn't...

I hope no one's taken you to a bad place.

I hope where you are,
you're happy being there.

I just want to know that...

would you let me know...?

if you could

show me

something

so I know...

I'll wait...

    (Silence...)

(For some time, nothing but silence...)

(... and darkness...)

(... except for that one red lightbulb...)

(It's so hard to see... it's very hard... but it seems possible that something... some kind of presence might be in the room...)

(... but that could also just be the room tone... or the sound of the lightbulb humming... do lightbulbs hum...?)

(... or maybe our eyes and ears are playing tricks on us...)

(... but it does seem like there's an odd shadow in the back...)

(and something definitely made a sound...)

hello...?

(Silence...)

*(**HILDA**, speaking to the audience...)*

something had definitely entered the room...

and Linda started having one of her spells.

*(**LINDA** begins wheezing – she's having an attack.)*

(She uncovers herself.)

*(**HILDA** admonishes **LINDA**.)*

Shhhhhhh

no, stay under there

*(**LINDA** gets back under the sheet.)*

…it was just…sitting with us…

sitting by Linda…

I don't know if she could tell.

It stayed with her for awhile.

I can't tell if it was just watching her

or if it was, in some way, feeding on her

or…

I wondered if I should do something.

I wondered if I should try to ward it away,

but to be honest, I didn't want to attract its attention.

If it was feeding on her, better that it feed on one person

instead of two.

And after some time, the thing left.

And we waited some more.

And at a certain point, I decided well I guess that's it

(The stage lights flick back onto full as the red light flicks off.)

*(**LINDA** remains covered.)*

That was the last time I ever saw Linda.

She doesn't answer my calls.

I can only guess why –

maybe she grew tired of me, or

maybe she was mad at me for taking her to my
mother's place when she wasn't feeling well

or maybe she experienced something that night,
something real and just felt too embarrassed to
admits she was wrong and I was right,

or maybe that night she just slipped through
to the other side – ha –
or <u>maybe</u> I slipped through – ha ha – maybe <u>I'm</u>
in the other place now.

I don't know. Who knows anything really…

some people believe in a world beyond this one,

some people believe there's nothing

and some people believe in things like God or science or –

and who's to say who is right.

It's just so easy to make yourself see
what you want to see –
That's something Linda taught me:
we see what we need to see,
and it really is just the most wonderful thing

because it means we're all "right" in a way,
right?

> *(Shrug.)*

I don't know
I just like to keep an open mind about these –
I'm sorry but –

(Catching the eye again of that audience member from the top of the play.)

it's just the funniest thing
how much you look like my grandmother.

Oh I wish I had a picture I'd show you – I mean
It's just such a coincidence it <u>must</u> mean something, right? I mean
it just makes me wanna –
I really just wanna –

(...Fishes out a pad of paper from a side table.)

(And she writes something down on the pad.)

*(And then **HILDA** starts laughing to herself as if from embarrassment...)*

(Then composes herself.)

okay, just
just just –
all you have to do is listen
just
really listen

are you listening?

…

…

…

Do you hear the word I'm thinking of?

(The audience member does not hear anything.)

No like really listen

...
...
...
...you heard it didn't you.

> *(The audience member actually hears a word in their head.)*

What word did you hear?

> *(The audience member says the word they heard.)*

> *(And* **HILDA** *just gets the biggest, happiest smile on her face.)*

Yeah,
that's it.

> *(***HILDA** *turns the pad around to face the audience, and it's the word the audience member said...)*

That's –
That's just the funniest thing.
That's just the funniest –

> *(***HILDA** *is just so happy, so serenely blissfully happy.)*

> *(And* **LINDA** *–* **LINDA** *who's been standing this whole time under that sheet upstage –* **LINDA** *starts to move, like she's about to do something, and that moment the sheet falls –* **LINDA** *is gone.)*

> *(Lights snap out with a cloud crack.)*

> *(The play is over.)*

www.ingramcontent.com/pod-product-compliance
Lightning Source LLC
Chambersburg PA
CBHW071838290426
44109CB00017B/1855